SUMMARY

Preface: forgetting common meanings of *good* and *bad*.

Preamble bis

Almost all interests in which people lose their way is *vanity*. A great part of zealous jobs to which the masses from different walks of life dedicate a big part of their lives wouldn't deserve so much effort.
So far…
But what pushes a contemporary man so inexorably towards the *emptiness? Boredom from abundance? Fear of commitment?*
As far as boredom is concerned each century showed its remedies and for now let's leave them out not to make our demanding reader *bored*.
The fear in itself, instead, is a double face feeling.
It sets traps for those who experience it in a passive way, but benefits a lot the one who knows how to profit from it.

If we associate a person with the term "good", what are we thinking about?

Here is the list of adjectives describing a good man: *altruist, sensible, empathic, tolerant,* generally inoffensive.
Just in one word, *Moral.*
And in other words: *loyal.*
But to what? To *status quo.*

The morals are to some extent the expression of the society.
Let's take as an example the "social solidarity".
Would this value be ever possible in the society where there is no poverty? Of course, not.
In contemporary societies – just as in the past – the values were not born *naturally.*

The Power creates and promotes values functional to its continuity and survival. The *Base* is shaped with them not having a valid counterpower to depend on. But the Mass with its conformistic values, disconnected in itself, can do nothing against the cohesion of Power.
Conformism, therefore, represents the road suggested by the establishment which the Mass must follow, otherwise there will be a *public moral conviction* or *repression.* There are no alternatives.

For example, who can permit oneself today – political party, opinion leader or just a citizen – to challenge capitalistic society without a risk of isolation?

Right and *Left* in politics have never been so close before in the Western world. Never before have they offered so similar solutions to the problems. For this reason, in the USA, the turnout is attested by rather low percentage and a bit over 50%. There is no real alternative to this kind of society.

The morals, in the course of the centuries, constituted a valid instrument to alleviate the fears of Mass and Power, representing a point of reference, an unquestionable certainty to which different behaviours conform in view of the? common good. But also an extraordinary instrument of social control. A good at service of *Justice (lat. Iustitia, Ius=law),* with consequent *security* of individuals – in the religious extent of the concept, the *salvation* for individuals – and of the established power.

The *ignorance*, in general, is itself? execrable and causes inappropriate behaviours producing *disinterest* or *interest* in the matters of little value. The ignorance of moral laws – not formalised in a code but written in the conscience – is a deplorable thing in the eyes of the mentioned Mass. It leaves "non-conformist" men at the mercy of everything, knocking on ungovernable whirlwind of life and its situations without any remedy.

Far from these lines therefore, to erect new destroyers of morals or false heroes. Instead, we analyze and criticize an approach to life. Predisposed. Scienter induced and functional.

All around we have a proliferation of: *'Scandal!'*, "Scoop!", "Incredible!".

Then you turn to look at them asking where is the scandal behind the events of "gossiping" in which everybody participates with enthusiasm?

The real scandals are different!

"Summer stories" cannot have such a big specific importance on people's lives.

All these interests are idle practice, facilitated by Boredom of well-being and alienation. Good.

For Boredom, everyone is free to find his own solution. Where you can – and you must – act is on values. You have to dig a lot in order to reach the point. It is not easy, indeed, to pull down cultural fundamentals settled through the centuries. Really arduous then, when everything seems to go in the opposite direction. But there is no alternative: the awakening goes through the *pretending to know*.

Good men of former times

The term *kalokagathia* is a transliteration of a Greek expression (καλὸς κἀγαθός, kalòs kagathòs, καλὸς καὶ ἀγαθός, kalòs kai agathòs), which describes the union of two precise elements of value: *beauty* and *goodness*. With these terms in the Hellenic (culture) – but also in the Roman culture – the ideal of human perfection was indicated: the union of beauty and moral values in the same person, a principle that involves the ethic and aesthetic sphere and also widens its influence on the Hellenic art.
Apart from that, kalokagathia broadly speaking indicates the real fusion in the ancient Greek culture of ethics and aesthetics; according to which what is beautiful must be good for sure and vice versa.
As a consequence what is *bad* inside will also be *ugly* outside. In respect of this fact we remind – right from Nietzsche – the critics of Socrates as *ugly*: *"It's well known, and you can see even today, how he was ugly. But ugliness, in itself an objection, is among the Greeks almost a refutation."*

In mythology *Achilles* perfectly reflects the Greek concept. Exactly the opposite is represented by *Thersites*: a simple soldier – *ugly* and *chicken-hearted* – a social antihero par excellence, who appears in the part of Iliad when Agamemnon is trying to convince his soldiers to go away from Troy, but Ulysses interrupts everything and convinces the soldiers to stay, disagreeing with *Thersites*. Between the philosophers who studied the field of ancient morals analysing the developments and deterioration, Nietzsche is in the first place.

He states:

260

We should notice at once that in this first kind of morality the opposites "good" and "bad" mean no more than "noble" and "despicable"—the opposition between "good" and "evil" has another origin. The despised one is the coward, the anxious, the small, the man who thinks about narrow utility, also the suspicious man with his inhibited look, the self-abasing man, the species of human dogs who allow themselves to be mistreated, the begging flatterer, above all, the liar:—it is a basic belief of all aristocrats that the common folk are liars.

This means that the only ones who are in charge of dictating the right values to the society are those who belong to the dominant elite. Everything they do is *good* and *beautiful* not much for the results, but because of the author. In this case, the paradox that an aristocrat and common people perform the same action and the judgement would be different becomes true. Nothing new under the sun. It also happens nowadays.

Again:

"Noble and brave men who think this way are furthest removed from that morality which sees the badge of morality in pity or actions for others or désintéressement [disinterestedness]. The belief in oneself, pride in oneself, a fundamental hostility and irony against "selflessness" belong to noble morality, just as much as an easy contempt and caution before feelings of pity and the "warm heart.""

That is an aristocrat, the only one who was authentically moral in the past until the Christian caesura (real "Copernicus revolution" of the morals), is not minimally and naturally projected towards the others, to whom he applies a proud "pathos of the distance". He neither founds his own actions on the disinterests – a hypocrite – nor on the compassion – contrary to *modesty* – (*Thus Spoke Zarathustra: A Book for All and None*), but rather exclusively about him. He himself is the moral.

Ultimately, which logic turned over the status quo?
"The slave has an unfavourable eye for the virtues of the powerful; he has a skepticism and distrust, a refinement of distrust of everything "good" that is there honoured—he would fain persuade himself that the very happiness there is not genuine. On the other hand, those qualities which serve to alleviate the existence of sufferers are brought into prominence and flooded with light; it is here that sympathy, the kind, helping hand, the warm heart, patience, diligence, humility, and friendliness attain to honour;" (F. Nietzsche, Beyond Good and Evil, in complete Operas, vol. VI, pp. 186-88).

The point is: the morals "of the slaves" that Nietzsche defines as the biggest lie, do not pursue the happiness of the man, but his *'domestication'*. The man with these morals is a half man, mutilated of Dionysian that is inside him. That moral, as mentioned before finds its fundamentals in Christianity, is the cause of current *decline* – a "give up" to nth power – in which the individual just like a domesticated slave does not know how to struggle anymore neither for what he desires nor for what he is up to.
This is today's picture that, starting from far away, Nietzsche was able to foresee more than a century ago.
However, that God who the German philosopher thought as dead transfigured, producing these results: *resignation* and *renunciation, acceptance* of status quo and *conformism*.
Or rather, a *modern good person*.

These outcomes represent extraordinary instruments in the hands
of someone who possesses the power and they allow elites to
exercise smooth control over the masses. Those seem asleep, lost
in the myriad of distractions and purely Christian belief in
unavoidability of the things. Something like: sleepy renunciation,
instrumentum regni.

Monstrum

How does the modern good man look like?

He is a mix of diluted *Christianity* (also called "modern") and shining publishing *marketing,* immersed in "the society of the look" and in "the logic of consumption". The synthesis for which the stock of values of the first – revisited in the modern key – matches the demands of the latter: a product of the contemporary society.

A real *monstrum,* if analyzed with old categories (*renunciation, forgiveness, love for the neighbour*) cannot stand still, but it holds well. Just because old categories have been updated. Even keeping the old diction, now they mean something else.

The keystone of the system is a widespread *well-being* without which the *scaffolding* would stop to perpetuate.

But let's come back to our monstrum.

The economic system weakened the resistance of the institutions in charge of the transmission of social values – religions, media, economy and the state in primis – dictating them its logic.

The continuous production of un-*essential* needs, merchandising of the values – "*you are what you have, you have what you are*" – an exasperated and irritating research for innovation in a key of productivity (the latest model of the mobile phone, the newest computer, etc.), the dominance of the *appearance* over the *essence* invested the spiritual institution which in order not to fade was slowly adapted. Fastening themselves to the process in progress. Whose "genetic mutation" of the religious phenomenon is exemplary.

The pontificate of John Paul II, the most pro-media pope in the story, is a good example of that and shows the situation very well. The figure of a Polish Pope, elected in general scepticism "through the intercession of the Holy Spirit", represented a caesura.

He transformed the figure of the bishop of Rome into a real "star of the Christianity" – once more showing how economic component is dominant. He managed to put *sacrum* over *profanum*. Just through marketing he brought the Church closer to young people and to believers in general, making the message more effective. He attuned to the frequency of the contemporary society through a smart use of *gesture* and *word*. As far as his work is concerned none of those who still admire and miss him remembers nothing (except for his battle against communism).

To tell the truth, as a Head of the Church he was but a revolutionary as many claim.

With him, the Church becomes a material entity in the eyes of all believers, taking defined and family characteristics: from *Pope* he becomes *papa*. Once beyond the reach, now can be touched. This is the end of the process of "commercialisation of the faith" in *democratic-commercial* key ongoing for years: the continuous spot in which the goods advertised are not from heaven anymore, but tangible and available to everyone – not mentioning the flourishing trade emerged everywhere near the places of worship, where you can buy all religious symbols, holy pictures, rosaries and much more.

It doesn't matter if Jesus Christ drove all the merchants by whipping them out of the temple. Other temples.
And other times.
Today, the Spirit made himself with flesh and material.
This is a purely advertising logic, to show repeatedly, repeat continuously to attract the customers and make them buy something.
In this case what do the *believers now customers* buy?
Values, comfort and hopes.
They store them up just as any other consumer goods, filling in the spaces without meaning.
That is just thanks to the *market* – to its rules and logic – so also the religion found the way to last. Selling the soul to the devil and giving one *sense* to the system, no matter how credible.
It is the "ideology of comfort" that mitigates the anxiety of the modern society from senseless hyperactivity and that fills with the substance a reality which has assumed the characteristics of a hollow shell.
Notwithstanding the appearance – *de facto* – politics, economy and religion row in the same direction. They clash, enter into debates with the only objective: to find a more useful compromise for themselves.
The preferred instrument to use is always the same: the *Mass*.
The politics addresses the voters.
The economy the consumers.
The religion the believers.
It is always about the Mass, regularly exploited and manipulated to get power and control.
But if *Power* points to calm us down (through distractions and misinformation or official information), in fact, making us *lose interest* in things that are worth knowing and about which we should worry, it must be said that the determinant role is played by a widespread welfare – not by accident the real obsession of the *establishment.*
Without it, the whole building would risk seriously collapsing.

Two bodies, double morals: the *monstrum*

The myth: the sovereign nation governs through its representatives.
The reality: the politics governs through people representing their interests to perpetuate and survive.

Let's go on to analyze more specifically the main actors. We will use 2 old, but effective categories: the *Power* and the *Mass*. Graphically, Power and Mass can be represented as the antipodes in the Mayan pyramid: the Mass lies on the large base while the Power is hoisted to the summit, where there is no real vertex, even if it is far more limited than the base. The two bodies – complex but more homogenic than they seem – may vary in extension.
The first is elitist and is animated by logic not at all democratic, considering that the members are practically *predestined* – from the day they were born – or enter in co-option.
The second, immense, comprises all those who are not members of the first one.
Using schemes we can say that the Power is composed – but only at maximum levels – of the following sectors that penetrate each other.
There are 5 main branches of Power that are strictly connected with each other:

- economy
- politics
- media
- religion
- secret organisations

What makes them connected?
Convenience, of course. And reciprocal *blackmailing*.
Apparently rivals, but, in fact, now allied, cooperating, ready to support each other in case of threat against the common cause.

Economy...

The politics and economy are interconnected, with the latter in a dominant position over the first and able to direct all others (also religion, *supra*) – as a hidden financier that strongly influences the programmes and lines of the government.
The politics lives from financing and what should we expect from the governments if big *corporations* strongly support them?
On which base can we plan a real election programme and to whom should we account for before than to individual voters?

The last ones decree the election results on the basis of a superficial programme. In reality they unconsciously endorse the interests of one or other hidden financier.

And if – as it often happens in the USA – there are weapon-business multinationals that support a candidate, how can we possibly think to avoid war?

Instead of reading the official programme of a party, the voter should investigate the hidden financiers in order to understand where his vote may go.

In a kind of limbo – neither inside nor outside the Power – the big media represent the "official voice" of the Power and serve as a sounding-board to several motions. They communicate what is allowed, omit what is inconvenient: the *official truth*. They determine under dictation the agenda of topics that should be given to the Mass. Then it is said: this is a public opinion. But what kind of reliable public opinion can you have, if you do not know all the facts? If you are in front of uncertain facts or effects produced by unknown reasons, what will be the result? A public opinion maimed and disoriented as well as interpretative chaos, according to which everything is true and its opposite. This is just what Power counts on. Where the manipulation does not arrive, arrives silence. A doubt, in fact, is the best ally of Power as far as it splits, divides.

Religion today (with a particular reference to the Catholic Church) – exceeded the historic problem of cult freedom and terminated this way the phase of opposition to the constituted power – follows everything but spiritual. It is an economic machine full of tax-free properties and with a dynamic financial business.

A real economic shark.

It is also beneficiary from state financing in every part of the world, besides the enormous donations from the believers.

Just like economy, it makes pressure, conscious of being able to move a remarkable number of votes, in one or other way.

There are plenty of examples of this practice in Poland and in Italy, where the politics, hoping to win the elections, has to agree with the clergy.

The secret organisations are the only ones that do not need *advertisement,* as they operate deep underground, making from this *total secrecy* their strength (let's not concentrate too much here to name the role of masonry in the formation and management of the national states).

They can cement various sectors of the society, recruiting the members of one or another. An emblematic case is "P2", freemasonry lodge that recruited crosswise from the sectors of public life representatives of the first level: from politics to culture, to secret services, police and army as well as to a legal system and business world. One of them is Silvio Berlusconi. Another monstrum having a secret plan, very precise and detailed, called "a democratic Renaissance". And what about CIA? Its role in many obscure affairs on the global – overturn of governments – and national scale, not least the death of Kennedy?

Therefore, even if apparently the politics, economy, media, religion and secret organisations may seem in a perpetual conflict, in fact, they finish to act together - *e pluribus unus* - towards a common objective: the growth of power through fair compromises.

The impact of these convergences affect the mass – out of the game, determining nothing – according to the old logic of *arcana imperii.*

As another example of these compromises, think that *"Benedict XVI in his encyclical letter from 2006 titled 'Deus caritas est' says that apostolic notice to share everything is impractical in the modern world and that, as a consequence, the Christian community does not have a duty to give indications on the social justice, but must delegate a question about the responsibility of governments"* (Comune. Oltre il privato e il pubblico, Negri, Hard).

What at first sight seems to hit a wrong note with the intervention of the Church, sounds like a laconic *do ut des.*

This is called: "don't stamp on somebody's toes".

The politics of *arcana imperii* considers legal for the Power what is not for the citizen and then it has to take the decisions in secret to avoid scandal.

The two social actors play, therefore, an asymmetric game. This entails two points of view on the reality of facts and consequently two different morals, two languages on the antipodes.

The power, strong in structure and knowledge, follows the interests of elite and mostly obscure, through so-called *reasons of the state.* It acts with *realism, rationalism* and *manipulation,* which accompany those who are in the high part of the pyramid. It has a clear vision and without filters on the situation produces the reality with its own acts and can convince everyone beneath it. Therefore, it is correct to say, Power lives in *truth,* because it creates it, being itself an author of deeds (and misdeeds), measures etc.

On the contrary, the Mass lives in lies ("filtered truth" or *official* as you wish to call it), as the deeds of Power fall on it without possibility to avoid them or at least help producing them. The morals according to which it must live – founded on altruism, sensibility, tolerance etc. – apply only to it, being feasible only in the base of the pyramid. It is the daughter of lies. It perpetuates in lies.

With the Mass one lives in the state of substantial ignorance – induced or voluntary – and in the indifference from *divertissement* which the Power ensures as never missing. It is thus divided, disorganised. Following the individual needs, suffering from *sentimentalism* (which religion helps to instil and from *laziness,* the daughter of passivity): it is the army of a *good man.*

Bad Person and the context

We call *bad* all those who cannot recognise themselves in the immanent system of values in the Western societies and who see as a cause of reigning *do-goodism* a substantial *softening of the reason.*

This softening – first of all, a child of widespread material welfare, but also of *impotence* to determine something – produces a constant disinterest for important things: the triumph of *divertissement* and critical disengagement.

The widespread *ignorance* of the facts, in its big part scienter produced by elites is one of the principal causes of the process.

"Not knowing" determines *a general alienation from reality* and the birth of collective moral completely *marginal* (valid only for the Mass, being the Power completely released).

The problems become insolvable puzzles for which it is not worth to lose head: better to lose interest. So now the reason and passion meet in prefabricated worlds organic to the Power: *information* and *entertainment.*

Information is full of gossip, crawling with irrelevant, gross news and is subject to censorship. Let's think about what happens during the political debates.

Each section denies the numbers of the other one!

Not only about ideas, arguments and solutions to the problems, but also mathematics! Something that should never be a matter of opinion.

The entertainment gained such industrial and capillary dimensions to become the fundamental axis of the man's life. Let's think about football and about the unbridled passions that it arouses. There are people who would die "defending" their club colours. There are other people who really sacrifice – economically – just to take part in sportive *actions* of the preferred club.

Abnormal extension of entertainment (sport and television) and proliferation of new media "in a distracting key" describe well the *panemetcircenses-isation* of the society.

At the same time, from the phenomenon mentioned above, it is chilling realizing the emptiness that must be filled in thanks to these tricks.

The strong point of elite (economic and political) is in the fragmentation of the masses. The Mass is confused, scattered, unable to organize itself. This is on what the elite bases its strength. Basically, it is a limited circle, an organised minority, structured and conscious of its role that pursues precise aims and maintains its power easily. From this point of view, democracy and socialism are nothing but myths to feed the masses that reveal what they really are: hollow shells, utopia only good for

manipulation of the masses, making them believe in power that in fact they do not have.
Most of all, it is a clever method to obtain *legitimacy*.

Mosca together with Pareto, the founder of "the theory of elites" at the beginning of the 20th century, proposed the criterion of three C's to describe the mechanism: *Consciousness, Cohesion, Conspiracy*.

The members of the political class are aware of their common political, social and economic positions and the state of fragmentation of the masses.

Despite the masses, the members of the political class join allies and organise themselves.

Finally, the members of the political class disguise their government to the mass, they hide the fact that there is an elite in power.

Confronted with all this, also *the bad ones* – or good in a different way – are the minority not organized. They are aware of some set-up tricks from Power and are in open debate with it, critics, rebels against those who want us tamed, disinterested and softened.
The *meanness* is a "modus vivendi", an alternative approach to the facts and life situations that can cost isolation and mockery.
The tendency to stigmatise those who do not line up is a common fact of all times. It's the remedy preferred by cultures, societies and governments to save themselves.
The application of negative value judgements (real signs of infamy) to people, things or facts was, for centuries the most typical trick of Power to fight against the "other" as *a non-conformist, deviant* and *dangerous*.
We all are always in a regime of *brain washing*. But fortunately, it does not work in the same way for everyone.
Those more combative are aware of the sophisticated mechanism that is behind the Mayan veil, understanding the hidden manipulative structure. On the contrary, good men, like blindfolded, carry on to neglect the evidence, babbling about freedom, inalienable rights, equality – convinced that all that is guaranteed. They hang on every word from the mouth of the "official truth".
From their side the bad men, discovered trickery, oppose and fight with all possible measures.

Everything starts from conscience.
The conscience of manipulation to which we are systematically submitted already imply passing to a higher level.
However, in a kind of reversal of the world, today the one who knows – or at least who hears different bells ringing makes an alternative opinion – in the eyes of those who are fed with the

official rumours, he is deplorable: it is a *conspiracy man*. He is *dangerous*.

It is the *stigmatization* and the allergy to the differences sprouted from the softened thought to ask for a ready sentence.

Bad person, aware of his solitude, laughs with pleasure at those who love singing always the same "chorus".

"We are connected because we are equal, we share the same sentiments, the same interests" – they affirm proudly.

The concept of equality – between the masses – often comes back: in reality it is a convenient forcing. The evidence is plotting against them.

Bad person perfectly knows that there is no equality in nature – if at all, exists hierarchy or at limit similarity.

Of course, not always in the *difference* must be considered the opposition superiority/inferiority. But just the term – difference – in itself disavows equality that is a "mythical" principle on which the Western civilisation is founded.

Bad person hates lies and that is why he condemns the values on which the society is founded. He considers everything the mass loves of little value. A hidden direction caused that people almost completely focused themselves on the useless and on work, becoming in fact the slaves of the 21st century.

Leisure and work. Work and leisure. In due distance from the knowledge, the reality of facts and ultimately from the causes of all joy and pains.

Who decides what must be the common good?

The elites, or really few chosen people. Today, just like yesterday.

Everything changed in the course of centuries to make no changes at all.

In reality, the pursued common good is nothing but the interests of few that rarely coincide with the one of everybody.

And when it does not coincide they make it coincide with lies.

"Manipulation" and "systematic introduction of disinformation" contributed to create an agreement for the most controversial operations of the recent history.

Let's take the war in Iraq in 2003.

There was a painstaking preparation before the attack through the media. The propaganda was prepared for months, the Iraqi regime was shown as a threat for humanity, able to trigger off the third World War.

They worked on the emotions of people, creating alarmism in order to justify a military attack to the public opinion. We even managed to invent that the weapons of massive destruction were present in Iraq – the decisive accusation able to shift the remaining scepticism on the operation. An accusation then became clamorously pointless.

Therefore, the war was declared on the basis of false accusations. This is only one example of the strategy adopted by Power to impose its will on Mass, controlling the agreement.

A marvellous synthesis of *manipulation, disinformation* and *control*.

The control, a basic element that makes use of the first two.

Let's take a *Patriot Act*, approved the day after the 11th of September. The generalized disinformation – scienter fulfilled – favoured the approval of this measure. The climate of terror fell down on the Americans, completely hidden from the causes, generated a substantial agreement. The human rights organisations revolted against the liberticide, understanding that the controversial measure involves:

- the decrease of citizens' rights
- the violation of privacy
- the decrease of freedom of expression

Before a verdict of the District Court of New York (judge Victor Marrero, October 2007) declared unconstitutional the *National Security Letter* – scheduled in Patriot Act – it was given to FBI, CIA and other authorities of public security to ask for wiretapping and internet traffic to the provider, without a mandate from the court and a notice to the direct interest of the material acquired.

Ignorance and terror, therefore, are between the preferred means of Power to control the masses and operate with a generalised agreement.

Thanks to ignorance and "time bomb" terror it was possible for Bush administration to put in place one of the most incredible plans for the limitation of national   (*Patriot Act*) and international sovereignty *(Doctrine of pre-emptive war)*.

The Doctrine of pre-emptive war is nothing but the manifest of "a new world order" made in the USA, inaugurated by George W. Bush Jr. with these words:

"For much of the last century, America's defense relied on the Cold War doctrines of deterrence and containment. In some cases, those strategies still apply. But new threats also require new thinking. Deterrence, the promise of massive retaliation against nations, means nothing against shadowy terrorist networks with no nation or citizens to defend. Containment is not possible when unbalanced dictators with weapons of mass destruction can deliver those weapons on missiles or secretly provide them to terrorist allies."

(A speech to cadets of West Point, 2nd June 2002)

A disorganised mass – as mentioned before – is more or less unconsciously at the services of elites that forever in the story pursue their objectives, and to achieve them the masses always constitute a mere instrument.

Bad person avoids this logic. He tries not to be used by any means, contrasting the passivity of others with the activism.

Exercises the reason, analyzes, informs about the causes, asking himself continuously "why?".

In short: he is a *plotter*.

The instruments that the moral furnishes the mass with are not for him, who passionately wants to know, without distracting or taking refugee in comfort that the society is ready to assure him at any time.

He says: "comfort and renunciation are refugee for the impotents".

Bad person is a crazy variable that threats the system. He does not recognise at the base of the pyramid any *justice*, because it does not foresee any *truth*.

By truth we intend:

The knowledge of the causes that are the origins of significant facts for the society.

Without it *justice* cannot exist, because the facts fall on the head of people without possibility of right interpretation, discovering the responsibility.

As a consequence the reactions of the mass cannot be nothing but instinctive and/or steered.

And rolling between half truths or entire lies it is hard enough to serve *justice*. A lot easier to serve for the interests of others – as the model *war in Iraq*. Always absent-mindedly.

The society of welfare and distraction

The social structure in the contemporary West has a form of a
Mayan pyramid. The pyramid from vertex cut at the top, where
neither the king nor the Egyptian pharaoh sits, but a group of
powerful men, mainly from the field of economics, politics,
religion and occult.
At the base, clearly larger, there is Mass.
There lie the good, more distant from the headquarters of
decisions and from the truth: they are controlled better and,
therefore, less dangerous.
Today, more than in the past, the concept of mass prescinds from
the social class of membership and it starts to become even more
a transversal fact.
Today belonging to the mass means to have the lowest level of
information at disposal and to be deprived of conscience, almost
far away from the reality.
It means being cut out from reality of facts and, therefore,
surrender inexorably to the own destiny of subjects.
The control over the mass becomes easier thanks to the
widespread welfare that states again the supremacy of economy
in all social dynamics from the top to the bottom and vice versa.
At the logic of having, bends also a religious authority.

"With Benedict XVI – writes Gaetano Quagliarello – *there is less
distinction that for a long time has justified a political
intervention of so-called "catholic reformator". There is no
more* before *and* after*: there, in no capitalistic process that
provokes injustice and? catholic reformator, who slowly has to
act to fix it; on the contrary, between political and economic
acting a full integration is necessary."*
The *having* favours perpetuation of *status quo* and the self
reinforcement.
In different sectors the market produces a huge quantity of
consumer goods that expect only to be bought.
Their peculiarity is expiry date: everything expires, not only food
products, but also indestructible shoes or clothes in perfect state,
if not new.
The *expiry date* of goods decrees the productive process –
always more persisting – that continues to produce without
thinking about the real needs of people. They are producers,
suppliers of goods on the market who decide about our needs.
Away from any hypocrisy, not even too low, contemporary
Western society considers decent only a life that meets consumer
trends, giving life to a constant psychological violence until more

people can live comfortably with these trends. Who cannot follow is *out*.

Think about TV commercials.

They offer models to follow 24 hours a day, they send subliminal messages that modify our way of thinking, values and ultimately also our behaviour.

The excessive power of capitalistic economy – that while describing monstrum we put in the first place – transformed the citizens with their rights into consumers of goods.

The Power knows that the force is strictly associated with satisfaction of material needs, trivial as often as not. The impossibility from large stripes of the population to grab the goods poses a threat, a source of instability.

If happiness consists of having, not of being or knowing, they provide until everyone is put in the condition of possession.

The possibility to pay with infinite instalments a "custom-built car" or a "dream holiday" keeps up the appearances and gives the illusion of happiness, because it helps to feel in the harmony with values the society promotes every day.

In reality, the needs we are induced to satisfy *put to sleep*, *weaken* and *distract*. They move the target, come prefabricated only to increase the supremacy and control of elites on the vertex of pyramid: accomplice and instrument of Power. As a consequence, the Mass spends a big part of their existence on understanding how to grab those goods the society obliges them to suck, while searching for *welfare*. For whom is lying at the bottom of the pyramid it coincides with the possession of *goods*. The happiness and the possession of goods then coincide and Power cares that those come bestowed in big quantities – and if possible with average prices.

The life of those who aspire for material goods as "a main road" to happiness is a mechanic life and disinterested with affairs that occur in the high spheres of the society. Bombarded by entertaining messages, Mass lives from *entertainment*.

> *"I see clearly that you will make some men happy, by diverting them from the prospect of their domestic distresses, and making them apply all their care to become excellent dancers."(B. Pascal,* Thoughts, *S. 348-352)*

Keeping away the hidden actions and the scopes of Power from the majority of population through manipulation of the news, the filtered truth or the silence is not enough. Power prefers to be sure that the Mass stops being interested in the things that happen upon their head. Stressing the control.

There come to scene the so-called "weapons of mass distraction", various, expressions of the system and managed by the system, ultra applied by capitalism. According to the country and its relative structure there are different forms of distraction.

In general, TV represents a "diamond point" of the "distractive apparatus".

In Italy, a country where people read very little (without considering *free press,* the newspapers distributed in underground and elsewhere), according to the official statistics released by *Prima Comunicazione, Corriere della Sera* and *La Repubblica* – the biggest national daily newspapers – in the period between October 2009 and September 2010, did not even sell one million copies altogether (442.141 copies the first one, 413.836 the latter). They are daily newspapers that include between their lines names of the first quality, opinion leaders, financed by big sponsors.

Going behind the ocean they read more. In the USA – where, in fact, daily printing is more variable and multiform – we find *The New York Times*, with more than a million copies sold.

Let's go back to Europe, to Great Britain. Here we find *The Sun*, with around 3 millions copies sold.

In Germany, we have *Bild* that with 5 millions copies is a best-selling daily newspaper in Europe. It's noteworthy. But it's nothing compared to the power of TV. To intercept, in the world, 90% of people who do not read we have TV. Also in the countries where they read more, none of the medium has a penetration like TV or radio. Another discourse should be devoted to the web, potentially able to supplant "the magic box", and the development of multimedia system that incorporates more communication means in a single support.

But let's stay with the traditional. Each medium has its peculiarities, in general, widely destructive and/or manipulative.

In the first part of the 20th century radio played the role which now is taken by TV. Totalitarian regimes of Nazism and fascism found radio as an extraordinary weapon of consensus and propaganda.

German minister of propaganda Goebbels has foreseen in the *repetition* of determined messages an extraordinary technique of persuasion for the masses. The same technique was adopted by advertisements. Apart from means of propaganda radio also guaranteed entertainment. That is distraction and for the transitive property, control.

Today, when entertainment – together with culture – became an industry, sport, film, variety shows in industrial quantity, games with prizes making people dizzy are present 24 hours a day. The reality shows are like daily bread for the Mass that follows them almost religiously as if they were something unique. They become a subject of discussion and support. Just like Big Brother, the triumph of *voyeurism* and *uselessness.* Entertainment fills in the life of people who dedicate themselves to it with an absurd seriousness.

Let's think about attention that a simple sport event is able to spread. A soccer game in Europe, basketball or football game in the USA.

Sport entertainment is capable of triggering off violent passions, joys, pains and rage, sometimes unrestrained.

A real safety valve for a great part of users, if not channelled in futile causes could represent an important risk for every establishment. Especially because of this, regimes of all times have endowed that for the masses entertainment and distraction would never lack.

In Italy, in 1948, even seemed that the victory of the cyclist Bartali in Tour de France conjured a revolution after an attack on Italian Communist Party (PCI) leader Togliatti.

Besides, as mentioned before, at the base of the pyramid, we live in a parallel world in which other logic is in force (illogical, sentimental).

The world in which *lies* reign, where you react *irrationally* and *sentimentally* (as certified also the triumph of "TV of pain") to the more or less dramatic facts happening and which are the causes of other people's final acts and decisions. In the total darkness where the majority of people is forced to move, here the surplus and the instrumental become a "point of reference" to which to cling on.

The heroes of the mass are false, not real. I do not mean the characters, but what they represent, for what the mass considers them as such. They simply fill in the emptiness, the space scienter left free, full of omissis.

In the acts of the "protagonists" of the "industry of distraction" there is nothing heroic.

What is so heroic in a football or basketball player?

And what in a participant of Big Brother or in a Hollywood star? Really nothing.

Or rather, the illusion of having a relation more or less direct with those *icons*, together with a certain proximity due to the availability of very detailed information (this is not censored, but favoured) mark absolute success of the mass distraction. For all the advantage of Power that as a small minority would never be able to exercise its supremacy having constantly eyes on itself.

However, the power of distraction even if evident, is not absolute. As mentioned before, the welfare favours the perpetuation and the reinforcement of power. Violent economic crisis would strongly loosen the power of distraction.

Also because the access to the channels of distraction becomes really impossible. Being distracted costs and who cannot afford it represents a threat. At a point, one should almost pray for this blessed crisis.

Disinterest and Renunciation

What cannot be seen, what is far away, is not interesting. Or rather it does not exist.

The distance between Mass and Power is an example.

At the base of the pyramid arrives nothing but a twisted echo of the facts that happen at the top. If it arrives at all.

Welfare and *distraction* work as a sleeping pill, produce alienation, increasing de facto the hiatus between the summit and the base.

As mentioned before the mass lives in another world, an artificial one, obeying logic functional to Power.

A forced distance from the truth inexorably produces disinterests.

A general disinterest that absorbs conscience of people pushing them to occupy themselves with trivial things most of the time. What the Latins called *otium* – a moment of amusement, a rest from daily activities – becomes the salt of their lives, the only reason to live.

Work, revenues from work are nothing else than a good way to pay for leisure.

Liberty granted by money, for the Mass, is a liberty to divert one's attention from the reality of facts, staying away from the decision table, with no regrets.

Disinterests at the base produce the ignorance of facts and actions performed by Power. We are not talking only about voluntary ignorance (that substantially is *renunciation*), but of a real difficulty to reach the truth.

Because the monstrum about which we wrote at the beginning, a composed elite entity, is at the same time a *producer* and *distributor* of the news, so it is able to change the truth, how and when he likes according to its own consumption.

So aggression in Iraq, from an ordinary petrol war against the sovereign state (shamefully governed as you wish to call it), becomes almost a heroic act of charity marked by the slogan "let's export democracy".

The masses have never been the authors of anything. When everything goes well they are unconscious co-authors.

Normally, an instrument.

With this key to the reading easy enough to understand how the worst vileness in the story of the 20th century happened with and thanks to people's acceptance.

Hitler arrived to power thanks to free elections. Nazi party – out of any hypocrisy – had a big part of *Volk* on its side even when declaring that Jews are the inferior race. The advertising technique of Goebbels gained the following.

Fascism in Italy was welcomed with a noteworthy consensus from 1924 until 1940, greeted by the vast majority of Italians with enthusiasm.

This means that normally the masses cannot do much themselves, without having a comprehensive and truthful picture of facts in front of them so then they are an easy prey for manipulators.

Knowing the facts *ab origine,* would allow the mass to go back to the reasons, while status quo admits that only unknown facts are falling on it.

Going back to the reasons, in fact, one could look at the *responsibilities,* forming this way a *critical conscience.*

Mass conscious of the manipulation, aware of the origin of evil, aware of tricks played on its head and of all vileness perpetrated behind its back, would be a time bomb ready to explode and able to overcome everything and everyone.

Excluded from the world of *reason* – where it is possible to discern thanks to the knowledge of causes and effects – in the dark about *truth*, the mass lives in the darkness of lies and reacts instinctively to the stimulus received in a similar way to the dogs of Pavlov.

It is clear that, contrary to what Marsilio Ficino claimed – *Power must come from the bottom* – Power falls on the Mass, forcing constantly to provide the base for *work* and *entertainment* (Work x Entertainment = Welfare).

These components alienate the Mass from taking part in the management of a "public thing" and obtaining these goals becomes easier for the Power.

"Democratic fiction" enters the scene, given that Mass was silently dispossessed of any power.

In the symbology of the 19th century, an absolute sovereign – in reality Leviathan – was considered a Father of his own Nation, underlining from this perspective the emotional component of the existing relation with the nation.

Extending the significance of this relation, Power of any political form, always considers Nation as a baby. The baby that does not have to know everything (would not understand) and when throws a tantrum – or to anticipate – is given a toy, a time killer to calm it down.

In this scholastic way, the sovereignty is all along taken off.

Also in democracy, the same choice of representatives comes through a number of predetermined and constricted options. They are *oligoi*, few, those who are called to represent. The *selected ones* are in reality *pre-selected*. This is, in fact, an oligarchy and that is why we talk about a "leading class": a real oligarchy, a monstrum over which, intertwining of powers strictly connected with each other.

All this does not seem to disturb much the Mass that even if aware of this subordination accepts it as an inevitable condition.

From a dangerous entity, a prey to beastly instincts, the Mass was tamed. It became *good*, inoffensive.

And if oligarchy with power will be able to furnish *work* and *leisure* to overabundance, they can stain of the worst injustice without anyone realising it and, even realising he rebels against it.

The stomach is full, go to hell responsibilities, injustice, abuses. We do not know them, they do not exist.

We discover them? They don't bother us. Feet apart between the vertex and the base of the pyramid is such that sometimes the indifference continues, also in the moments of crisis. And as crisis we intend material crisis, i.e. the loss of work and ability of buying.

Other kind of crisis does not bother the Mass: does not exist. Demographic crisis, hunger in the world, games or several abuses of power do not find a space on the agenda of common people.

Official information filtrates also those questions defining them as low interests threshold.

We can see that *disinterest* in reality of facts, more than an inclination of Mass is a product of Power, the monstrum mentioned above. It is a son of continuous work of Power separation from Mass that represents, in fact, the divestment of sovereignty of those who lie at the base of the pyramid.

The lack of access to the truth stops the individuation of responsibilities and with that the formation of critical thought and of conscience at last analysis?.

One lives in the cave. Direct consequence of disinterest is *pardonism* or *justificationism*, as you wish to call it.

With stomach full, disinformed, manipulated, the Mass forgives everything: corruption, overuse of power, abuses.

Living in the "golden cage" weakens, until getting up out of all proportion the threshold of tolerance (for injustice and abuse).

Let's take Italy, the country where the distance Mass - Power is a paradigmatic example of all Western democracies.

In spite of the institutional and economic crisis the country is going through for the last 15 years, the citizens are inclined to *pardonisms*. The elections show very low abstentionism, despite the scandals of all kinds (from those financials model Parmalat to the political model Tangentopoli), and inefficiency of political class that earns having no equal in the West, in front of the falling revenues of the citizens.

In Italy, the relation with Power is of medieval kind.

For the leading class, more than to lead, is legal to command.

The citizens – especially from the South of the country – have the relation with power in a kneeling mode. They become indignant, sometimes bark, but basically forgive, understand and renew their trust in the representatives participating massively in every election.

As far as unacceptable privileges of politicians are concerned, G.A. Stella and S. Rizzo in 2007 published a book titled "La

Casta=The Cast" that was a quick diffusion and provoked a big disdain among the citizens. TV transmissions start to give space to the topics and politicians, plied with millions of questions they engage themselves to do something to reduce their rewards. After few months, their engagement finishes, we do not know anything and a thundering silence falls on the matter. Neither newspapers nor TV takes up the question and Italian politicians as usual remain still privileged.

Of course, if media do not say anything, interests decrease, indifference diminishes and the problem remains.

Generally, in Italy we assist one "wonderful" example of the "introduction of disinformation".

It seems that certain data do not exist. Everything is possible to interpret, even the statistics (everyone quotes his own reliable sources). This produces disorientation that is almost impossible to go back to *cause, authors* and *responsibility*.

As a consequence, people vote exclusively on the basis of support and not on the basis of conduct, positive or negative as it is.

The chaos reigns sovereignty and in chaos the Power gets stronger. That induces the Mass to misleading and fatalistic generalisations of the type: "politicians are all equal".

It follows a substantial resigned indifference for what happens in high spheres of the society that is nothing other than the renunciation of one's own sovereignty. Because, if somebody who has the power is allowed to do anything just because he has the power, the concept of democracy is being completely deprived of its meaning and reduced to a simple *mechanism*.

A common mechanism, like an acclamation of the boss or an election on census basis can be. A good method just like any other to appoint uniquely the "representatives of a nation".

In Anglosaxon countries, as well as those post-Communistic of Europe, *disinterest* is manifested in another mode: with *abstentionism*.

We can claim then that the distance between Mass and Power in the West produces a different kind of disinterest, depending on the culture and costumes of the single society.

In the USA, where basically people vote very little, the sexual scandal cost Clinton a presidency, forced him to step down because he lied to the Americans.

In Italy, following the polls, Berlusconi accused of graft and child prostitution did not seem to lose support.

These are diverse declinations of a unique phenomenon: indifference.

In Poland, the sexual scandal of Lepper (a bit later committed a suicide in mysterious circumstances) – a leader of Self-Defence Party – practically signed the end of his party and his leadership.

Do not make you lead astray because of the fall of Clinton and Lepper.

The political end of the two, in fact, was determined not by a motion of national contempt, but by decisions coming from the high level, ridden from media that as usual is one of the arms of the monstrum. Moreover, the two respective countries constitute a paradigmatic example of disinterest in the West. It is enough to think about the statistics of affluence to the votes: abstentionism, in fact, reaches from 40% to 50%.

Definitively, it is evident that the continuous exposition to multiple sources of distractions and the inaccessibility to the key information establish disinterest and alienation.

The *addiction* to the indifference leads irreparably to renunciation.

The renunciation is a mental condition which lacks completely the will to change status quo, also the most compromised. A real refusal, dictated by detachment and impotence. A kind of fatalism for which everything that happens is inevitable and so useless that it is not even worth taking care of.

It is a final result of weakening of the Mass, the triumph of control and domestication of the "beast": the mass of renouncers coincides with good men. Good men, the biggest success of Power.

The mission of bad person

There is a myth that explains better the difference between a *good* person as we mean it here, an individual from the mass, sleeping and distracted, nourished with lies and alienated, and a *bad* person as we mean it in this essay: the allegory of the cave.

"Let us imagine some individuals who live in a subterranean cave, a cave in which the opening is toward the light whole of its breadth, with a steep ascent; and let us imagine that the inhabitants of this cave are bound hand and foot and neck in such a way that they cannot turn their heads around, and hence can fix their gaze only on the black wall of the cave. Let us imagine then, a fire behind the prisoners in front of which is a walkway and behind the walkway are men who carry on their shoulders images, statues made out of wood, stone, and other materials, which look like all the kinds of things that exist.
....
Let us imagine, finally, that the cave has an echo and that men who pass beyond the wall speak to each other their voices bouching around and producing an echoing effect.
Consequently, if this were so, these prisoners could not see anything except the shadows of the statuettes that project on the black wall of the cave and they would hear the echoes of voices; but they would even believe that these echoed voices were truly the voices produced by these self-same shadows.

Now let us suppose the one of these prisoners arises and frees himself from his bonds. Then, he would with great difficulty habituate himself to the new vision that appeared to him; and being habituated, he would see the statuettes moved above him on the wall and understand that these are more true than those he had first experienced and that now appear as shadows.
And then let us suppose that someone takes our prisoner outside the cave and the ramp. He would be firstly blinded by the light; then having become habituated to it would begin to see the things themselves, first in their shadowy appearance and then in their reflections in puddles and pools of water. Finally he would see them directly, as well as the sun, and understand that only these are true realities and that the sun is the true cause of all that which he had seen." (A History of Ancient Philosophy: Plato and Aristotle, By Giovanni Reale, John R. Catan)

Frees himself from yoke, once escaped from the politics of calming down, bad person unburdens everything heavy that pushed his head to the ground.

This is a white fly on which the process of domestication was not successful.

Escaping from control, the bad one, diverted and deviant is a source of concern for the *monstrum* (and its *subjects*): it is dangerous.

Given that none of the techniques used by Power defeated Him, "plan b" started: the discredit.

So bad person is labelled by Power as undesirable, deviated, conspirator, insane. In practice, a public enemy that establishment tries to discredit in various ways, to avoid the spread of virus.

Not least mockery.

In talk shows, for example, in the rare cases when journalists or experts from different sectors are invited to spread "counter-current truth", we see the best the techniques of mockery.

Sniggering in the background, jokes, disbelief of the kind reserved for an insane.

After 11th September 2001, we had a perfect test. Transmissions after transmissions in the whole world have dedicated to this topic hours and hours of debates and who cast the doubts – more than legal – on the dynamics of the facts that the official communication transferred on us, not only was mocked, but also pointed out as a criminal.

The force activated by Monstrum to avoid epidemic finds anyway a fertile ground in Mass.

The public condemn of ideas – when not explicit, subliminal and underground – that goes beyond the barrier of official truth is practically a verdict ready to be received by people. Who thinks basing on the categories that socialisation from the top gave them and responded to a precise stimulus. The mass, however, is by DNA very sensitive to the number. And if out of 10 people, 9 think in one way and 1 in another, the credit is given to those 9 without even listening to the reasons of the 1st. Which automatically becomes *strange*, *bizarre* or even unpleasant. They do not have neither will nor time to dedicate, taken as they are from their practical pre-occupations connected principally to 2 spheres: *duty* and *pleasure* (meaning work and leisure).

Everything that takes up time for these two components is useless for them, does not deserve attention. How can we imagine that in this logic (promoted in all ways by Power) would ever be a place for a careful analysis and a search for truth.

Bad person places himself in a secure distance from all tricks of Power.

We do not have to consider it as a stylite, detached from reality and isolated. On the contrary, even if immersed in the reality he is able to keep his critical sense, maintaining this way his autonomy.

He also makes use of *leisure,* but he knows how to distinguish the moment and above all the instrumental function.

Also for this, he is careful, difficult to be manipulated and able to analyze facts and news, going back to their origin. It is a huge business for the bad one, par with the one of Prometheus.

The myth of Prometheus, after the one of the cave, describes efficiently the role of bad person in the society, its function – undesirable – and its peculiarity, especially in relation to Power.

"Once upon a time, the gods existed, but mortal creatures did not. And when the destined time of their birth came, the gods formed them within the earth, blending them from earth and fire and from those things which are formed by being combined with earth and fire. When they were about to bring them into the light, they appointed Prometheus and Epimetheus to embellish them and distribute to each the appropriate specializations. Epimetheus begs Prometheus to let him make the distribution. "And when I have finished, you inspect them." And so he persuaded him and began the distribution. But since Epimetheus was not all that clever it escaped his notice that he had used up all the special talents. Left unprovided still was the human race and he was in a quandary what he could use(...)

In this paragraph, the difference between good (Epimetheus) and bad (Prometheus) emerges clearly. The etymology of names is an ulterior proof.

Epimetheus, or rather "the one who reflects late", thanks to its inexperience or forgetfulness – that we can see as a daughter of distraction – is the cause of bad things for all people besides himself and that assails the same Prometheus.

Notwithstanding, in the myth of Epimetheus and Prometheus are demigods, so different from people, here we consider them two types of men: good and bad (in Mass).

Their actions, if applied to the Mass have opposite effects: if we are like "the one who thinks late" – or does not reflect at all, neglected absent-mindedly in the "game of exemption" – we remain naked, defenceless at the mercy of events.

Instead, if we are far-sighted – as Prometheus – we get to a superior level of conscience, able to defend ourselves and foresee better the adversity.

"In a quandary what means of survival he might find for the human race, Prometheus steals from Hephaistos and Athena technical skill with fire—for without fire it was useless and could not be acquired—and gives them to mankind. In this way, then, the human race had skill for living, but they had not the political art. For that was in Zeus' hands. And there was no time for Prometheus to go into the acropolis, the home of Zeus. And besides Zeus' watchmen were awesome. He did go in secret into the

common workshop of Athena and Hephaistos in which they practiced their crafts and stealing the art of working with fire from Hephaistos and the other art from Athena he gave them to mankind and from this the human race got the means of living. Later because of Epimetheus, [322] as the story is told, Prometheus was prosecuted for the theft."

(Platone, Protagora, 320 C - 324 A)

Made impotent from distraction, deprived of conscience and ignorant, the Mass cannot do nothing but distract itself, putting *sense* and *passion* into all undeserving activities. Bad person – Prometheus – to avoid this diversion wears thief's shoes. He robs powerful people of their resources (techniques, knowledge) and gives them to the unaware. And for this he pays not for his own mistakes, that Power – from its point of view – attributes to him. The one that strips off the Power of its means that give it superiority, becomes guilty and so he must be punished.

"Prometheus came secretly to the fireplace of Zeus, probably to the fireplace in the Olympian palace of the gods. He took and hid the spark in the hollow stem of a shrub of narthex and waving it not to let the fire extinguish, while satisfied he was running fast between men. To Prometheus, Zeus reserved a memorable punishment: he bound him to a mountain in the Caucasus and appointed an eagle, the daughter of Typhon, to eat during the day his whole liver that was growing again during the night."

To unmask the Power, to decrypt the codes and give them to the Mass, "bad" Prometheus adopts the same logic, learns how to speak the same language.
Robs and gives.
But the Power cannot accept it and that is why it punishes Prometheus for the serious offence. The Power has to stay untouchable and inaccessible *de facto*, but appearing close, almost within hand's reach.
There are basically 4 duties of bad person:

1) *bring closer*
2) *inform*
3) *attract*
4) *restart the dialectics*

Point 4 is consequential.
After the renunciation, the critical spirit died, the Power enjoys a kind of consensus in the dark. Only by bringing closer, informing, attracting the Mass the extinguished dialectics Mass-Power can be reanimated.

Distance, disinformation and indifference have produced *renunciation* that deprived the Mass of any will to change status quo. Restarting the dialectics means, moreover, awakening the *will*. A will to oppose, a will to fight for a change, a will to take part without "blank delegations".

Means at disposal

The task of our Prometheus is arduous.

He is not a demigod, he is just a man armed with conscience for whom no darkness has come and where the politics of *calming down* did not worked out.

The will is alive in him and he heroically continues an unbalanced struggle against the Power, constantly trying new allies, with an objective among others: resurrecting the dialectics.

His motto is: **"the will to know is power"**.

But how to cope with that in the jungle of steered news, omissions, manipulations, small talks and silence?

How to cut out a "space of attention" in the middle of myriad of distraction that keep people's life busy?

How to shake out the critical sense *paralysed* by the Mass?

How to redirect the curiosity of the Mass towards the right objectives?

Bad person starts from the axiom that the official truth is *not truth* considering that, as truth, it would not need at all the official blessing.

Here, we deal with a masked lie.

Finding a way through very disparate news about the same fact, our Prometheus tries to make a critical analysis, going back to the origin, pinpointing the causes and responsibilities.

He searches for truth.

He refuses official versions and draws on many sources.

He considers pluralism as richness, as the main road towards conscience.

Internet is his strongest weapon. It is an ideal territory for those who search for truth, a place for discussion, a field where the manipulation finds it difficult to produce effects. But it is also an *"anarchic territory where everything can be said without contradictions"* (Eco, The False and the True, L'Espresso, 5th May, 2011).

Aware of everything the bad one continues under the heading of The Will to know is power.

But which power?

The power of not being manipulated.

The power to self judge without being "routed" by others.

The power to control those who are at the top of the pyramid and to ask for explanations.

In general, we can say that the positive aspects of internet as an almost unlimited reservoir of information are a vast majority, compared to those negative.

Just think of one of many scandals in which Berlusconi took part: the one with the photos that show the Knight - and Czech Prime

Minister Topolanek "in the state of excitement" – in his villa in Sardinia together with various naked girls.

If the Italians counted on their national press to get to know something, they would be deluded: they would know nothing.

In fact, the censorship – preventive or imposed as it was – covered up everything.

Thanks to the web, it was enough to go online and see a Spanish daily newspaper El Pais to discover what happened.

Such an incredible unsaid scandal, able to turn pale Clinton's past, came to light thanks to the "internet power".

Extraordinary.

In illuminating *Media without mediators*, Michele Mezza describes how thanks to not so much futuristic technology (a mobile phone), individuals from recipients of news falling from the sky step by step became the producers.

And thanks to them, it was possible to transmit in TV unpublished images connected with important events of recent years.

From the attacks on Twin Towers through the tsunami of 2006 to the cataclysm that devastated Japan in 2011.

These events, documented by ordinary people having just simple cellphones, bear witness to the fact of dissociation from traditional media and potential competitiveness of an active citizen, producer of news.

Moreover, in case of images or facts captured they were supposed to suffer the burden of censorship of traditional media – supporters of the official truth just to clarify – it would be the network to run and rescue. Creating a *web page* where to publish a post or a video is easy and *youtube* platform is always available after registering your own account.

Bad person – like Prometheus – has human being in his heart. Then it is automatically in conflict with Power that feels justified to use it the way it wants.

As mentioned before, classical media, that really should orient, contributing to the training of conscience founded on truth, they disorient fully performing their ancillary function.

From his side, the bad one is the master of the web and the future seems to smile on him. The riots in North Africa, are said to be born from the network. Today, young people have almost maniac relation with internet and social networks, similar to the one that previous generations had with TV.

With a substantial difference that the "magic box" was – and is – totally in the hands of monstrum while the web is – for how long? – a free space.

If in China they apply filters and censorship also to the web, the turn that it could have in the West is worrying.

In America, you cannot be surprised of how Obama would "nose out the deal" using the web in his electoral campaign. Internet in the advanced West represents a new border. For now, in spite of the intolerance of Power holders that everything – and everyone

– wants to calm down, brings back to order and control, the web resists like an off-limits zone.

A new "public sphere".

"Born from the need for emancipation of liberal middle class, a «public sphere» is initially like a forum of opinions where the power of the best argument serves to control Leviathan and guarantees the rights of an individual. But in the society of mass communication, a public sphere is under structural transformation. Instead of a forum for discussion and critical comparison it becomes an arena where they probe, change place and manipulate opinions. So it transforms itself in mass media space where a consensus is produced and the society is controlled. And where they, instead of emancipation and freedom, have only their semblance. (Franco Volpi, La Repubblica, 2002).

A trial of Leviathan to hush up public opinion spaces, comparison, discussion and news is not so far to come. On the contrary.

In 2011, in a little European country, Hungary, a really "gag law" that seriously prejudices the freedom of press and the right of the citizens to be informed and to monitor the Power was approved. An authentic muzzle applied to the world of media tout court.

With a majority of two thirds, Hungarian Parliament, controlled by ultraconservative party Fidesz of Prime Minister Orban, gave life to a law on press with the following main points: the first is suppression of the news editorial staff for TV and radio, which would flood into one news centre at the national press agency Mti, financed by the State. The new law foresees big fines on information agencies in case of violation of a somehow flexible public interest, articles "politically unbalanced" or "detrimental to human dignity". The weight of sanctions (fines that start from 700 thousand euro for TV up to 89 thousand euro for newspapers and web sites) openly favours a kind of preventive censorship, that in fact discourages the publication of unpleasant news.

Furthermore, TV news broadcasts must respect a limit of 20% for the crime news and in line with the most classic of autarchic traditions, at least 40% of the music transmitted should be of Hungarian origin.

Finally, an icing on the cake. In short, the obligation from the journalists to reveal their sources for the motives of "national security" – this Carneades in Hungarian salsa – with investigation authorities allowed to analyse all their instruments and documents also before identifying an offence.

Between lethal penalties and obligation to reveal the sources, bye-bye scoop, practically, bye-bye news. The fact that it happened "only" in Hungary probably did not provoke necessary rumours, but it represents without any doubt a very dangerous precedent. It should be monitored.

In a much bigger country like Italy, UE co-founder, Prime Minister Berlusconi might have liked to get something from this act (but if he had done it, there would have been such a chaos which would have completely overwhelmed him) when in June 2011 – in the margin of the sonorous defeat in the local elections – he declared:

"There was an extraordinary claw of media, all the press and newspapers in an unacceptable way. So unacceptable that it cannot happen again: we will work in the Parliament because this cannot repeat. (Bucharest, G8, June 2011)

If "Hungarian" laws should spread like wildfire, the task of bad person would become really arduous and probably for a moment our Prometheus would be reduced to silence and sentenced to extinction.

Here our Prometheus has to make the "fire", apart from producing light on the hidden facts of Power, wakes up in the Mass "a sense of indignation" that represents a spark, the only way out of the circle of kindness.

"It is by indignation that we discover power to react against oppression and so the force to fight against oppression and so the power to challenge the causes of suffering. Manifesting indignation our most intimate nature revolts. (Comune. Oltre il privato e il pubblico Hardt, Negri, p.239)

A "sense of indignation" is, moreover, an indispensable element in the course that leads the conscience which is the main road to regain "extorted sovereignty".

"I authorise and give up my right of governing myself to this man, or to this assembly of men, on this condition; that thou give up, thy right to him, and authorise all his actions in like manner. This done, the multitude so united in one person is called a COMMONWEALTH; in Latin, CIVITAS. This is the generation of that great LEVIATHAN, or rather, to speak more reverently, of that mortal god to which we owe, under the immortal God, our peace and defence. (Thomas Hobbes, Leviathan p. 167)

Extorted – we said – because in contrast to what Hobbes claims speaking of Leviathan, the monstrum in question did not receive from Mass any mandate, but through tricks and deceptions disposed it of its right to know and because of that valuing its work, being proud or angry and, in case, getting rid of it.

Leviathan through its tentacles has hypnotised the Mass reducing it to unaware subjection, the worst slavery. Bad person can just snap his fingers, stopping the *trance*.

Assisted by others, similar to him, he must sweat a lot to revive interest soothed for a long time, then to throw a seed of doubt, pushing individuals to think.

Individuals, not Mass. An individual is able to receive much more when he is alone than while in company. That is because when he is with others he has to deal with different dynamics and contexts that reduce his receptivity, critical capacity and common sense.

Prometheus points at "de-standardized individual".

He points him because *"an individual in a group is subjected through its influence to what is often profound alteration in his mental activity. His emotions become extraordinarily intensified, while his intellectual ability becomes markedly reduces"*. (Freud)

De-standardisation is preparatory to the establishment of a "new social community" of thinking heads and aware, that could cross one time all experience of Mass, the reign of equality, conformism and subordination.

In order that from Mass, created to obey, par excellance subject to the control of Leviathan, we arrive at the awakening of individuals, who once conscious gather in a community that is able to oppose *authentically* to Power.

A community that finally places oneself in a position symmetric to Power.

Again the web offers a proof of this work. It is an ideal ground for this process of de-massification that produces receptive individualities, just because separated from *others* and from *contexts* that would be concerned to share with others.

As mentioned before, those contexts have dynamics that we are pushed to obey, otherwise the exclusion arrives. One of these is identification and goes through *conformism*.

For a solitary individual, instead, in front of its PC, social links are loosened, the others – and their judgement – are far and it is simpler to be oneself, different and independent. We are more open to the messages "out of the chorus", more prepared to examine without defensive need to reject them.

The mechanism that steers to please others, in respect of common sense, is weak and virtual.

Eminent intellectuals – relegated to "index of bad masters" – through their blog put on the clothes of Prometheus. One of them Noam Chomsky, *"together with Marx, Shakespeare and the Bible, is one of the ten most quoted sources in the history of culture"* (The Guardian).

In his "factory of consensus" he lifts the "Mayan veil" describing the symbiotic relation between media and governing establishment to the detriment of the right information and then of the formation of judgement of news recipients:

"A propaganda model has a certain initial plausibility on guided free market assumptions that are not particularly controversial. In essence, the private media are major

corporations selling a product (readers and audiences) to other businesses (advertisers). The national media typically target and serve elite opinion, groups that, on the one hand, provide an optimal "profile" for advertising purposes, and, on the other, play a role in decision-making in the private and public spheres. The national media would be failing to meet their elite audience's needs if they did not present a tolerably realistic portrayal of the world. But their "societal purpose" also requires that the media's interpretation of the world reflect the interests and concerns of the sellers, the buyers, and the governmental and private institutions dominated by these groups."

It means: apart from a simple consumer, citizen-mass is the last wheel of the cart. Information, an optional.

Other worthy men like him, write about facts that official media censor, criticising without too much compliments men with power, examining their work – quite often criminal, unmasking fraudulent systems through articles and documents of opposite information.

They create opinions, throw a seed of doubt, instil an interest – also where they try to practice a scorched earth policy – and they find favour. They are always emulated from younger thinking heads that create their blogs, talk about taboo topics, starting discussions, confronting each other.

And the "malice" spreads. In the communication era, the will to know infects more people despite "the industry of entertainment" continuously churns out new mischief.

Thanks to the web, then, we start to catch a glimpse of an embryo of community of "thinking heads".

The powerful amount of information – true or false as it is – (in the jungle of internet the nonsense is always behind the corner) must have as a first and strictly connected task to reanimate the discussion between people, going to construct a valid alternative to the official sources.

This is already a fact. Even though the official institutions of information arrived heavily on the web, the world of web is so big that this is just a drop in the ocean. The alternative, unusual and in one word *politically incorrect* dominates internet and always feeds young people in a more substantial way, and ultimately the individuals that are more familiar with technology.

The hope to revolutionise the relation Mass-Power goes through the youth and technologies.

The web united the world and – doing so – multiplied the circulation of news, the news themselves and their recipients.

The structure *pre* "world wide web" was a separated and vertical structure. Each society had its own institutional system of information, through which the respective Power exercised its control on the respective Mass.

The structure that arose is instead composite and horizontal just because it is *world wide web* and it allows to undertake a path – through discussion, to the above mentioned trace of causes and responsibilities – that leads to awareness.

To reach that, we need to add to the *de*-standardisation – consistent in the effort to go out of common logic promoted and conveyed by Power through the "distraction apparatus" – the commitment.

As commitment, we need to undertake a severe research of truth, as an indispensable preamble in any type of attitude or action: either they are hostile or of consensus.

It is a titanic work that the sons of Prometheus have to embark to realise their desires of freedom and emancipation.

But the Power, strong in its extraordinary allies does not intend to give way.

That is why the rise of a strong *dialectics* between two opposites extremes, the Power – jealous of its prerogatives and its absolute supremacy – and that community of "thinking heads" that gets ready to become mass (of the bad) once again – involves *"the abolition of identity(...) This step implies also a violent clash with the established powers. The revolution is not for the weak at heart. It is for the monsters. You have to lose something in order to gain what we may become."* (Comune. Oltre il privato e il pubblico Hardt, Negri p. 337)

Conclusions

Leaving aside what happened in North Africa and generally in the Arab world – because it is outside of our area of analysis – in the heart of the Western world we have a clear example of what can happen when the policies of welfare and distractions fail.

The failure of these policies together with the substantial collapse of the economies had the power to wake up the numbest brains in the Western world.

Let's consider Greece, England and Spain.

In these Countries the illusion of an enduring prosperity (English case) or the mirage of a radiant future inevitable after the introduction of euro (Greece and Spain) made the awakening of the masses much bitter.

They catapulted them in a desperate scenario, a dead end, where the distraction is no longer possible, no longer the case, since they do not even have any material property.

Now the fire of the uprising, certainly benefiting from social networks, internet and the entire real-time communications, has been possible.

We had such an outbreak of indignation to warn not only the public opinion – official media – but also the top levels of politics.

The fact of the collapsing castle was indisputable. So it is equally obvious that a society based exclusively on practical criteria should inevitably collapse after the fall of these ones.

If you base the consensus on *having*, during a period of crisis the system shakes wildly.

They were few, unheard and boycotted Cassandras, those who proclaimed that Europe conceived this way would be dead at birth. Those who argued that it was wrong to build a brand new society over interest rates, inflation and state deficit, over banks and currencies, were pointed out for being conspirators and defeatists.

Actually they were right. They were right to suppose that such an ambitious project, which did not involve such a large number of citizens, was like building a sand castle.

Not only a strategic mistake in the light of the tragic results, but seems intentional.

Same logic, Same aims. In the secret rooms they decide independently. In public, they pretend they still have to decide.

So people take the bait.

Fortunately, not all of them, for example those bad men we have extensively referred to. They have not made themselves contaminated by the general enthusiasm, by the explosion of fireworks to celebrate what?

A single currency? For what? For the convenience to travel in Europe without having to change money?

The bad – well-informed – suddenly thought that everything must have a more complex explanation.

Moreover, they wonder why a single currency, the centralisation of economic-financial power has brought nothing politically significant in the same way?

Why did they make us join a new supranational player without explaining how and why, but only besieging us with rhetoric and illusions?

It's easy. They have already decided in the shadow of their rooms.

The financial economy – the strongest arm of the monstrum – has already decided what should have been, counting on the complexity of politics in order to take the burden of pulling the masses into the new castle.

The institution of referendum subject to an appropriate and detailed information campaign full of pros, cons and conditio sine qua would have been a must. However, some countries made use of it (with negative outcomes, though) while others did not.

This overtaking shows the idea quite well. It absolutely confirms that every "historical breakthrough" is guided. Once the doorway of a new path has been opened, the mass is cleverly made flown into.

Unless something or someone queers their pitch.

An economic crisis, a crazy factor, which can make his ghostly appearance either in Greece or in Spain, no matter.

Suddenly, we get indignant. With an empty wallet, farewell distractions, farewell dreams of glory.

Suddenly, everything becomes clear. The dialectics breaks into scene soothed by welfare, manipulation and diffused disinformation.

The reality cannot be hidden anymore. People immediately identify, connect facts, responsibilities and culprits.

It becomes indignant and reacts. In Europe and in America more mad people rail against establishment, fill in the squares and in some cases devastate everything they find on their way. Now, it is impossible to be entertained for more people who exceed the threshold of poverty.

The collapse of Western economies marks a beginning of a new phase on which we need to keep an eye. Increasing the control to nth power, informing oneself in all the available places about what the global Monstrum is going to do to face the crisis.

This is a key moment, like in the 20th century it was 1929 or the 70's, that preludes important social and political changes.

These phases of precariousness usually finish with wars and/or restrictions of freedom meant to strengthen elites in difficulty.

The manipulation and concealment of reality are the techniques preferred in these cases, but which are more difficult to implement today because of the pervasiveness of Wi-Fi information that allows everyone at any time and everywhere to get information. And if so, act.

But possible action can only be organised – and to be organised it must be conscious, of course not episodic or occasional.

If a citizen is an expression of society that he lives in, we need to strive for a better and fairer society if we want the future of superior quality.

But to do so we have to participate in this decisive phase of transition in which new arrangements that inevitably will produce new citizens are being prepared – but not for that necessarily better.

Of course they are functional to the interests of the authors of new arrangements mentioned above which aim to act undisturbed, out of any control of the masses.

This must be definitely avoided. But we are talking about a titanic work that weighs on the spirit of that "minority of bad men" that has a unique scope of spreading as much as possible their state of conscience through every available massmedia.

But time is short.

For the first time in the history of the Western world – excluding, in fact, the masses from decisive processes to overtake the deep economic and social crisis – we are assisting in the dismantling of democracy given that in this phase political elites have one fear: losing their power.